STEM
ON THE BATTLEFIELD

TORPEDOES, MISSILES, AND CANNONS
PHYSICS GOES TO WAR

Tim Ripley

Lerner Publications ◆ Minneapolis

Lerner Publications Company
A division of Lerner Publishing Group, Inc.
241 First Avenue North
Minneapolis, MN 55401 USA

For reading levels and more information, look up this title at www.lernerbooks.com.

Main body text set in Verdana Regular 11/16.5.
Typeface provided by Microsoft.

Picture Credits:
Front Cover: ©dragunov/Shutterstock,
Interior: ©Department of Defense, 1; ©Central Naval Museum St Petersburg, 4; ©iStock/Thinkstock 5; © Robert Hunt Library, 6; ©iStock/Thinkstock, 7; ©Boris Kisov/Shutterstock, 8; ©Spaxia/Dreamstime, 9; © Photos.com/Thinkstock, 10; ©Robert Hunt Library, 11tr; ©Robert Hunt Library, 11br; ©Robert Hunt Library, 12; ©Artur Bogacki/Shutterstock, 13; ©Jon Nicholls Photography/Shutterstock, 14; ©Shutterstock, 15; ©Robert Hunt Library, 16; ©National Portrait Gallery, 17tr; ©Robert Hunt Library, 17br; ©Robert Hunt Library, 18; ©Robert Hunt Library, 19; ©Robert Hunt Library, 20; ©Robert Hunt Library, 21tl; ©Robert Hunt Library, 21br; © Photos.com/Thinkstock, 22; ©Stocksnapper/Shutterstock, 23tl; ©Robert Hunt Library, 23tr; ©Robert Hunt Library, 24; ©Robert Hunt Library, 25; ©Robert Hunt Library, 26; ©Everett Historical/Shutterstock, 27; ©Department of Defense, 28; ©Robert Hunt Library, 29tr; ©Robert Hunt Library, 29b; ©Arterra/Getty Images, 30; ©NASA, 31tr; ©London Fire Brigade/Mary Evans Picture Library 31bl; ©Robert Hunt Library, 32; ©Robert Hunt Library, 33; ©Department of Defense, 32; ©Department of Defense, 35tl; ©Robert Hunt Library, 35cr; ©Orren Jack Turner/Library of Congress, 36; ©Atomic Heritage Foundation, 37tr; ©Photo Researchers/Alamy, 37br; ©Library of Congress, 38; ©Robert Hunt Library, 39; ©TAR-TASS Photo Agency/Alamy, 40; ©iStock/Thinkstock, 41; ©Department of Defense, 42; ©NASA, 43.

Brown Bear Books has made every attempt to contact the copyright holder.
If you have any information please contact licensing@brownbearbooks.co.uk

Library of Congress Cataloging-in-Publication Data

Names: Ripley, Tim, author.
Title: Torpedoes, missiles, and cannons : physics goes to war / Tim Ripley.
Other titles: Physics goes to war
Description: Minneapolis, MN : Lerner Publications, [2018] | Series: STEM on the battlefield | Includes bibliographical references and index. | Audience: 9–12. | Audience: 4–6.
Identifiers: LCCN 2016058433 (print) | LCCN 2017004773 (ebook) | ISBN 9781512439267 (lb ; alk. paper) | ISBN 9781512449549 (eb pdf)
Subjects: LCSH: Weapons—History—Juvenile literature. | Military art and science—History—Juvenile literature.
Classification: LCC U800 .R55 2018 (print) | LCC U800 (ebook) | DDC 623.4—dc23

LC record available at https://lccn.loc.gov/2016058433

Manufactured in the United States of America
1-42139-25412-4/3/2017

CONTENTS

PHYSICS AT WAR

In January 1878 Russian speedboats raced toward an enemy warship in the Black Sea. The Russians and their allies were at war with the Ottoman Empire of modern Turkey. The Russians wanted to gain territory on the Black Sea, which was under Ottoman control. The Russian speedboats traveled quickly. The guns of the Turkish warship *Intibah* could easily destroy them. The Russian crews used speed to get close enough to fire their weapons.

The Russians used a new weapon called a Whitehead torpedo. The torpedoes sped through the water powered by compressed air. They struck the *Intibah* below the **waterline**, and the ship sank. It was the first time small boats had destroyed a warship.

A torpedo blast sinks the Turkish steamer Intibah *as Russian speedboats wait nearby. This painting was created by the Russian artist Lev Lagorio Konstantin in 1880.*

SCIENCE SKILLS

The Whitehead torpedo was invented by a British engineer named Robert Whitehead. Whitehead was a skilled physicist. Physics is the science concerned with the nature of **matter** and energy. Physics has influenced weapons design for centuries. Physicists invented new kinds of bullets and **missiles**. They learned how to use the explosive force of gunpowder in weapons such as rockets. They developed new weapons such as the machine gun. Physicists have also studied how to use light, heat, and sound in warfare.

ENERGY OF THE ATOM

In the early twentieth century, physicists began to understand the structure of the atom. An atom is the smallest particle of a chemical **element** that can exist. Physicists figured out how to use atoms to create a huge explosion. The first atom bomb exploded in 1945. It helped to end World War II (1939–1945) and transformed warfare. It also changed the course of human history.

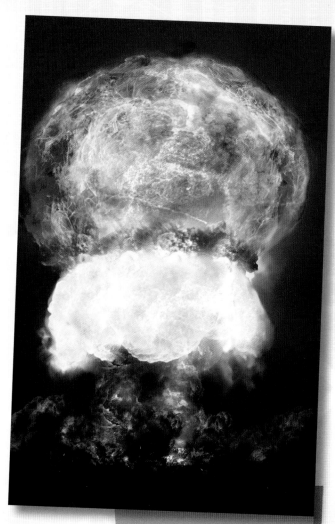

A fireball rises over a huge explosion caused by an atom bomb. A nuclear explosion creates a mushroom-shaped cloud as the force of the explosion pulls smoke and debris high into the air.

BOWS AND CATAPULTS

Bows and arrows were first used in the Stone Age. Native peoples in the Americas, Asia, and Africa continued to use bows as weapons until the nineteenth century.

The bow is a simple but efficient weapon. It consists of a bowstring tied tightly between two ends of a curved piece of wood. The ends of the bow act as levers. The archer's hand acts as the **fulcrum**. The archer draws the arrow back in the bowstring to create tension.

English archers (right) meet French soldiers armed with crossbows (left) *at the Battle of Crécy in 1346.*

When the archer releases the string, it propels the arrow forward. Bows create **kinetic energy**, so the arrow travels quickly and creates a powerful force. In the Middle Ages, when soldiers began to wear armor, an arrow with a steel tip could penetrate even thick metal armor.

ARROWS IN BATTLE

In ancient times, groups of archers on foot or on horseback fired hundreds or thousands of arrows at the same time. The rain of arrows they created devastated enemy troop formations. Then in the fifteenth and sixteenth centuries in Europe, archers used a new weapon, the longbow.

The tail feathers at the back of an arrow help it to fly straighter.

Catapults

Like bows, catapults use tension to fire projectiles. A catapult is like a long lever. Soldiers pulled down on the back to create tension in ropes at the front. When the throwing arm was released, tension whipped the end of the catapult forward and up. Catapults could throw rocks or burning materials against or over the walls of enemy cities.

The longbow was a weapon about 6 feet (1.8 meters) long. Its additional length allowed it to produce even more force than normal bows. Longbows took more skill to fire than regular bows because it was more difficult to pull back the bowstring. Skilled archers could hit targets from more than 220 yards (200 m) away. Longbows killed many knights on horseback because the arrows pierced their armor.

The long arm of a catapult was pulled down to create tension in the crosspiece at the front. When the tension was released, the missile was launched into the air.

The crossbow was far easier to use than the longbow. Nearly anyone could go into battle and fire a crossbow toward the enemy without much training.

THE CROSSBOW

Another common type of bow was the crossbow, which was invented in China in about 700 BCE. The crossbow consisted of a piece of wood with a short, curved metal crosspiece at the front. The crossbow had a mechanism to draw back the bowstring and to create tension in the ends of the crosspiece. The user fired the crossbow by pulling a trigger. The crossbow fired a bolt, a short metal projectile with a pointed tip.

Unlike longbows, soldiers needed little training to use a crossbow. The weapon was also easier to fire while riding a horse. The crossbow made it possible for commanders to move large numbers of unskilled soldiers who fought in huge masses. By the thirteenth century, the rise of mass armies marked the end of the era of mounted knights.

ARCHIMEDES' CLAW

Archimedes was a Greek scientist in the third century BCE. When the Romans attacked Greeks in the Mediterranean Sea, Archimedes designed new weapons.

Archimedes lived in Syracuse, a Greek city on the island of Sicily, near Italy. Romans attacked the city in 214 BCE. A Roman fleet of 60 large warships known as quinqueremes sailed to Syracuse. Archimedes had designed the city's defenses. As the Roman ships approached the harbor, the city's defenders used catapults to

Reports said that Archimedes used polished copper shields to focus the sun's rays into a single beam. The beam set fire to the wooden ships.

throw boulders and flaming missiles. The Roman ships rowed through the attack.

SPECIAL WEAPONS

Archimedes had placed other weapons in the harbor too. They included a "death ray" crane created from sunlight and "claws" on the harbor walls. These cranes picked up Roman ships and smashed them against the rocks.

Archimedes' weapons successfully drove away the attackers, but the Romans began a **siege** of the city that lasted for three years. The Romans finally defeated Syracuse in 211 BCE.

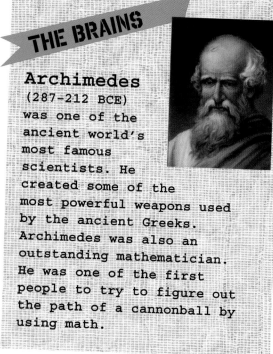

THE BRAINS

Archimedes (287–212 BCE) was one of the ancient world's most famous scientists. He created some of the most powerful weapons used by the ancient Greeks. Archimedes was also an outstanding mathematician. He was one of the first people to try to figure out the path of a cannonball by using math.

Archimedes built claws with large hooks that grabbed the Roman ships. A series of pulleys allowed the Greeks to lift the huge ships out of the water!

THE FIRST ARTILLERY

Muslims in Spain used the first modern artillery in Europe in the fifteenth century. The weapons would transform warfare.

The Moors were Muslims from North Africa who ruled southern Spain and Portugal. The Spanish and Portuguese went to war against the Moors in the fifteenth century. The Moors used cast-iron cannons that fired metal cannon balls. The cannon balls badly damaged Spanish and Portuguese castles.

Muslims surrender to Spanish soldiers after the siege of Granada in 1491. The barrel of a Spanish cannon lies on the ground.

In 1492, the Spanish defeated the Moors and forced them to leave Spain. But armies throughout Europe soon began to use the new gunpowder weapons. **Armorers** designed small weapons for use against enemy soldiers and large cannons that were used against **fortifications**. These weapons ended the age of large stone castles.

STRONGER BARRELS

The mass production of **artillery** weapons was made possible by new technology. Armorers made metal objects by casting, or pouring hot metal into molds. They were able to make cannon barrels in a single piece. The lack of any joints made the gun barrels stronger. This meant that the weapons could use more powerful gunpowder charges without danger of splitting open. Cannons could fire bigger and bigger projectiles.

Mortars and Bombards

European armies had special cannons for siege warfare. Mortars fired missiles in a very high arc. They fired cannonballs over tall castle walls so that the cannonballs fell on the defenders inside. Bombards had a large caliber, or barrel width. They fired huge cannon balls at castle walls. The balls blew holes in the stone walls.

Mortars had short barrels that could be angled sharply to fire missiles high into the sky.

GUNS AND GUN BARRELS

After cannons appeared in Europe in the fifteenth century, weapons makers began to develop smaller firearms. These guns could be carried and used by individual soldiers.

The Chinese invented the first guns in the thirteenth century. In Europe in the fourteenth century, armorers welded together iron rings to make barrels for small pistols or long **muskets**. Soldiers poured gunpowder into the barrel. They made a spark with a flint to light the gunpowder, and the weapon fired.

Soldiers with muskets lined up on the battlefield and all fired their weapons at the same time. This strategy killed or injured many enemy soldiers.

In the seventeenth century, gun makers rolled together larger plates of metal to make seamless gun barrels.

RIFLED BARRELS

Early muskets were inaccurate at long ranges, so rifled guns became common in the nineteenth century. Rifling was a series of spiral grooves made inside the gun barrel that made the bullets spin as they fired. The spinning motion made the flight of the bullet more stable. Small arms became far more accurate.

The shape of the spiraled rifling inside a gun barrel affects how quickly a bullet spins. Most bullets twist at least once for every 48 inches (122 centimeters) they travel.

THE FIRST ROCKETS

Rockets are long, thin missiles that contain gunpowder. They can reach great heights or distances. The first rockets were invented in ancient China. They resembled fireworks.

The first rockets were difficult to control and dangerous to use. The Chinese fired them at the walls of enemy castles. The use of rockets later spread to India and the Ottoman Empire.

When rockets reached Europe, armorers figured out ways to make them more powerful and effective. In the sixteenth century, the Italians began calling these powerful weapons *rocchetta*. The word meant "bobbin" or "little spindle."

This illustration comes from a German book about rockets published in the 1500s. It shows launching tubes and rockets flying in the air.

The weapons were the same shape as the bobbin or spool that held the thread for a spinningwheel.

TUBE LAUNCHERS

In the seventeenth century artillerymen launched rockets from metal tubes. They pointed the tubes toward targets such as fortress walls. The use of metal tubes made it safer to fire rockets close to one another without setting them all off. Eventually, armorers began to make rockets from the metal tubes. Gunpowder inside the tube exploded when the weapon struck its target. These new weapons were more accurate than earlier rockets and could carry more explosives.

William Congreve (1772-1828) was a British inventor. He built the first cast-iron rockets in 1805. The rockets had long sticks that helped them fly straight and were powered by gunpowder. Congreve based the rockets on weapons he had seen in India. British soldiers used Congreve's rockets during sea and land battles when Britain fought against France in the Napoleonic Wars (1803-1815).

This image shows William Congreve's rocket designs. The rockets with longer sticks carried heavier amounts of explosives.

17

ARMOR-PIERCING SHELLS

In the mid-nineteenth century, navies used metal plates to protect warships. Cannon balls could not pierce these "ironclads." A new type of weapon was needed.

Ship armor developed quickly. Monitors were steam-powered warships with sloped sides of metal armor. Missiles skidded off the sloping surfaces. Weapons designers tried to figure out ways to punch through this armor. They tried using rifled guns. These caused shells to fly faster through the air so that when a shell hit its target, it punched a hole in the armor. Shells with thin, pointed tips could pass straight through metal.

This Russian T-34 tank was destroyed by armor-piercing shells in a tank battle during World War II.

FIGHTING TANKS

The first tanks appeared in World War I (1914–1918). The use of tanks increased the need for armor-piercing shells. By the time of World War II, heavier tanks such as the **Soviet** T-34 appeared. Their thick armor could withstand hits from nearly any shell.

Scientists began to use very hard metals such as tungsten to create armor-piecing darts known as sabot rounds. In these, the shell case fell away as the dart left the gun. The dart struck an enemy tank at high speed, and the tungsten cut through the armor. In the late twentieth century, weapons makers gave sabot rounds tips of depleted uranium. Depleted uranium is one of the hardest of all materials. It made sabot rounds even more effective.

William Palliser invented the Palliser shot in 1867. The cast-iron shot was designed to penetrate armor on enemy ships.

Palliser Shot

The Irish inventor and politician William Palliser (1830–1882) designed the first armor-piercing shell for naval guns in the nineteenth century. It used a cast-iron case that narrowed to a point. A Chilean warship used Palliser shot for the first time in 1879. It sank a Peruvian ironclad.

SHOT RIFLED MUZZLE LOADING PALLISER.

7 INCH

VI

§ 2222

WEIGHT 113 ¾ LB± 1·5 PER CENT

CAPACITY FOR BURSTING CHARGE 1½ LB. IF REQUIRED

IRON MOULD

SAND MOULD

IRON MOULD

Over body 6·952 : 015
Over studs 7·31 : 005

THE FIRST TORPEDOES

A torpedo is long underwater missile with its own propellor. It explodes when it hits its target. This makes holes in the sides of enemy ships, which then often sink.

Navies have long tried to hit enemy vessels below the waterline. In the 1700s and 1800s, gunners on ships fired cannon balls at a low angle at enemy ships. The cannon balls bounced across the water and hit their targets near the waterline. Water flooded into the ships.

UNDERWATER MISSILES

In the mid-nineteenth century, engineers used compressed air to power underwater projectiles with explosives in the tip. The projectiles

These Argentine sailors were photographed with a Whitehead torpedo during a visit to Austria in 1888.

This painting shows the British ship Pathfinder *sinking after being struck by a German torpedo in September 1914.*

became known as torpedoes. A tank inside the torpedo released compressed air. The air spun a **propeller** to push the torpedo through the water. The invention of the torpedo transformed naval warfare. Small, high-speed boats with torpedoes could now sink or damage far larger ships.

The torpedo made its biggest impact on underwater warfare. Submarines could launch weapons without being seen by the enemy. The first time a warship was sunk by a submerged submarine was in World War I when a German U-boat, or submarine, sank the British ship HMS *Pathfinder*.

THE BRAINS

Robert Whitehead (1823–1905) was the British inventor of the modern torpedo. The British did not want the weapons, so he demonstrated it to the Imperial Austrian Navy in 1866. The first tests were not very successful. Whitehead worked on his design until it was perfected. For many years people called his invention the Whitehead Torpedo.

THE MACHINE GUN

Leonardo da Vinci, an artist and inventor, had the idea for a machine gun 300 years before the first one was made. Leonardo's weapon had many barrels.

The first machine guns were used in Europe in the mid-nineteenth century. Weapons such as the Belgian mitrailleuse had multiple barrels. The barrels were on the outside of a rotating cylinder. Each barrel fired as the operator turned a handle to rotate the cylinder. A single gunner could fire a whole **volley** of bullets.

French soldiers use mitrailleuse guns in 1870. The gun could fire bullets in a rapid sequence or in a single volley.

Hiram Maxim (1840-1916) was a British-American inventor. He embodied the spirit of the Industrial Revolution. He believed that it was possible to use technology to improve almost any aspect of life. As well as the first modern machine gun, Maxim built mouse traps, steam pumps, light bulbs, and circus rides. Every army had Maxim guns at the start of World War I in 1914.

The Gatling gun was fired by turning the handle at the back. It could fire 200 bullets per minute. Larger versions of the gun traveled on wheels.

NEW INVENTIONS

In 1861 the US inventor Richard Gatling invented a multi-barreled machine gun. The gun traveled on wheels, like a piece of artillery. The gunner turned a crank handle to revolve the barrels. The weapon loaded itself mechanically as the barrels turned.

British-American inventor Hiram Maxim invented the first true machine gun in 1883. It relied on inventions made during the Industrial Revolution. This was a period in the eighteenth and nineteenth centuries when technology led to the rapid development of new machines and manufacturing processes.

SCIENCE FILE

British sailors demonstrate a Maxim gun in the 1890s. The gun automatically ejected used shellcases.

Rates of Fire

The rate of fire is the speed at which a machine gun can fire bullets. It is usually expressed in terms of rounds per minute. Some machine guns have a fully automatic mode. All the gunner needs to do is pull the trigger once. As long as he holds the trigger, the weapon will keep firing. The guns can fire hundreds of rounds per minute.

SMOKELESS AMMUNITION

In the early 1900s chemists developed new ammunition for the machine gun. They invented smokeless gunpowder that was packed into a metal **cartridge** with a bullet. When the firing pin struck the cartridge, the gunpowder ignited. The bullet flew out of the gun, creating exhaust gas. A mechanism in the gun diverted the gas to push the firing-pin back into place so it was ready to fire again. The gun mechanism also moved the next round of bullets into the firing chamber. The bullets were usually held in long belts.

CHANGING WARFARE

Machine guns transformed warfare in the late nineteenth century. European powers fought **colonial** wars in Africa. A few Maxim guns could kill thousands of Native fighters, who carried spears and crossbows. During World War I the machine gun dominated the Western Front in France. It made it difficult for infantry soldiers to advance on the enemy. In the past, massed ranks of soldiers had advanced on the battlefield. The machine gun ended that practice as thousands of men died in any advance.

American troops train with machine guns in World War I. Machine guns caused huge casualties as soldiers tried to capture enemy positions.

DEPTH CHARGES

In World War I, the submarine became an important weapon. German submarines were called U-boats. They sank many British and American ships. Scientists invented weapons that could destroy submarines.

The first usable anti-submarine weapons appeared in 1916, during World War I. They were called depth charges. They were **detonated** by water pressure. Depth charges were not intended to hit submarines. Instead they exploded to create an underwater wave of pressure. This shock wave could break open enemy submarines.

Water Pressure

Depth charges use water pressure to destroy submarines. Submarines operate at great depths, where the water pressure is naturally high. A sudden increase in pressure or a pressure wave from a depth charge can cause a vessel's hull to bend. Joints and bolts burst open, and the submarine is in danger of filling with water.

In World War I, engineers designed launchers that threw depth charges about 45 yards (41 m) from their ships.

American sailors use depth charges to attack a German U-boat during World War II.

USING SONAR

In World War I, physicists developed sonar (sound navigation and ranging) to help locate enemy submarines. A sonar device gives off pulses of sound. It detects sound pulses reflected back from an object such as a submarine. Sonar made it possible to locate submarines accurately. It also made it possible to deliver a depth charge close to a target.

Another way to make sure depth charges hit a target was by firing several depth charges at the same time. Scientists also developed special fuses to make the weapons detonate at specific depths. That increased the spread of the pressure wave.

ROCKET LAUNCHERS

In the twentieth century, physicists designed new motors that made powerful rockets easier to make and safer to use.

Rockets had advantages over traditional artillery such as cannons. They were cheaper and easier to make and use, and could be fired more quickly. Some rockets also carried **warheads** that exploded in the air above their target. That meant that the weapon did not need to be very accurate. A rocket carries its own motor and guidance system. That means it can be fired from the back of a truck or from a flat railroad car. A number of rockets can be fired at the same time.

This is a preserved version of Stalin's Organ, a truck-based rocket system from World War II. It took its name from Joseph Stalin, who led the Soviet Union during the war.

MODERN ROCKETS

Modern rocket motors burn solid fuel rather than liquid gasoline. They can carry rockets thousands of miles. **Ballistic missiles** fly in a high arc into the air. At a set height, their motor cuts out and gravity pulls them down toward their targets. Modern armies use global positioning system (GPS) to guide their rockets. This allows them to hit targets with pinpoint accuracy from many miles away.

US troops in World War II fired rockets from weapons called bazookas. A single soldier could destroy a tank using a bazooka.

THE BRAINS

Clarence N. Hickman (1889–1981) was an American physicist. In 1941 he combined a small rocket motor with a high-explosive antitank (HEAT) warhead to create the bazooka. This rocket launcher could be carried by infantry soldiers and used to destroy armored tanks. The operator needed only basic training. Other countries created similar weapons, such as the PIAT in Britain, the Panzerfaust in Germany, and the Soviet Rocket Propelled Grenade (RPG).

29

FLYING BOMBS AND MISSILES

In 1942, the tide of World War II began to turn against Nazi Germany. The German leader, Adolf Hitler, asked German scientists to develop a new weapon.

The scientists designed what were called vengeance weapons. Vengeance means revenge. The weapons became known as V-weapons. After the end of the war, many of the scientists who had worked on the V-weapons moved to the United States. They used what they learned from designing the V-weapons to design missiles and rockets. Those rockets helped to start the exploration of space.

This modern photograph shows a preserved V-1 rocket at a World War II launch site in Normandy in France.

PILOTLESS PLANES

The first V-weapons used newly developed jet engines. The weapons carried automatic flight-control systems. They had wings, like airplanes. Each carried a 1,800-pound (850-kilogram) warhead. They had a range of 155 miles (250 kilometers) and could be launched from the back of a railroad car. The engine was programmed to cut out after a certain length of time. Gravity then pulled the V-1 down to fall vertically on its target.

V-1s caused great damage in London and other British cities. Once their engines cut out, V-1s struck targets at random where they fell.

THE DOODLEBUG

The V-1 was also known as the Flying Bomb or Doodlebug. It first flew in December 1942 at the Germans' Peenemünde test site on the Baltic Sea. The first V-1 entered service 18 months later. In total, the Germans launched 9,521 V-1s against targets in Britain, France, and Belgium. The V-1 later led to the development of the modern **cruise missile**.

A NEW WEAPON

Adolf Hitler was pleased with the V-1 and wanted to increase the number of missile attacks on enemy targets. He ordered his scientists to build a new, more powerful missile. The V-2 was the world's first ballistic missile.

When the V-2 was fired at long-distance targets, it reached an altitude of 55 miles (88 km) before falling back to Earth.

The V-2 had a range of 200 miles (320 km). It was fired from a mobile launch vehicle. From September 1944 to March 1945, the Germans fired 3,172 V-2s at targets across western Europe. The V-1 flew slowly and could be shot down by enemy anti-aircraft guns. There was no defense against the much quicker V-2.

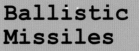

Ballistic Missiles

The V-2 was the first weapon to leave Earth's atmosphere. A powerful rocket motor propelled the rocket to the edge of space. At a set point, the motor cut out and the missile tipped back toward Earth. Gravity pulled the missile down at high speed. Tail fins on the V-2 were designed to control the descent. This helped direct the weapon to its target.

A V-2 takes off from the launch site at Peenemünde, an island on the Baltic Sea where Von Braun and his team tested the V-weapons.

Lasers focus light into thin beams. The beams can be used to measure distance, but they can also be destructive weapons themselves.

A US artillery sergeant uses a laser to highlight a target at night. This photograph was taken at night using night-vision technology.

Laser stands for Light Amplification by Stimulated Emission of Radiation. A laser beam can travel over long distances with great accuracy. This light technology led to the development of smart weapons. These weapons are guided to their targets by lasers.

An F-35 Lightning jet drops a laser-guided bomb. The bomb follows a laser beam to its target.

Lasers made range finders more accurate. Soldiers called spotters used lasers to accurately pinpoint targets. Missiles or rockets could carry small laser-targeting devices. The missiles directed themselves to their targets.

LASER WEAPONS

Several countries are testing directed-energy weapons. These weapons use lasers to generate great heat. The laser beam burns out the guidance systems of enemy missiles. It can also heat up a missile's explosives until the missile blows up in the air. Directed-energy weapons are fired from planes, ships, and armored vehicles. Other laser weapons are used to dazzle or blind pilots.

THE ATOM BOMB

The atom is the smallest particle of a chemical element that can exist. In the early twentieth century, scientists began to figure out atomic structure. They thought the atom might be made up of subatomic particles.

Scientists believed smaller particles in atoms contained large amounts of energy. They wondered if they could release that energy. They believed that releasing this energy would create a huge explosion.

EARLY RESEARCH

Scientists such as the German Albert Einstein and the Dane Neils Bohr researched and began to understand atoms. In the 1930s Adolf Hitler came to power in Germany. His Nazi Party began to

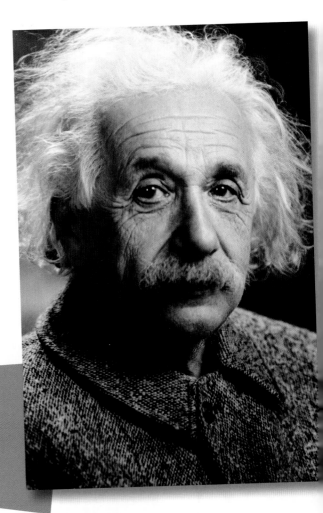

Although Albert Einstein supported building the bomb, he later said that it was so destructive it should not be used.

persecute Jews. Many Jews fled to the United States, including Einstein and other physicists.

SECRET PROJECT

World War II broke out in 1939. Allied politicians feared that German scientists would try to create an atom bomb. Such a bomb would be devastating. If Germany created the bomb, they might win the war. The Allies wanted to build the bomb first. They began a secret program to build an atomic weapon. The program was called the Manhattan Project. Scientists from the United States, Britain, and other Allied countries worked together on the project.

A fireball rises from the first test of a nuclear bomb in New Mexico. The Trinity Test took place on July 16, 1945. It marked a new age in warfare.

A CHAIN REACTION

An atom bomb works by starting a **chain reaction**. The chain reaction can be started in two ways. A trigger can split atoms. This process is known as fission. Or the trigger can crash atoms together. This process is called fusion. The Manhattan Project used fission.

The scientists planned to use enriched uranium or plutonium to power the bomb. These elements are called fissile. Their atoms were easy to split. An explosive triggered the fission process. As atoms split, they caused more atoms to split. The chain reaction caused a huge explosion.

The scientists figured out how much fissile material was needed to create a chain reaction. Enriched plutonium or uranium do not exist naturally. The scientists had to manufacture them from natural materials.

Little Boy was the atom bomb dropped on the Japanese city of Hiroshima in August 1945. It killed at least 70,000 people.

38

A mushroom-shaped cloud rises above the Japanese city of Nagasaki. The explosion on August 9 killed at least 39,000 people in the city.

The materials the scientists were using are **radioactive**, so they were dangerous to work with.

The first atom bomb test took place late in World War II, on July 16, 1945, in New Mexico. On August 6, an atom bomb was dropped on Japan. It devastated the city of Hiroshima. The bomb used uranium. Three days later, another bomb devastated the city of Nagasaki. This bomb used plutonium. At least 100,000 people died in the two attacks.

NUCLEAR DETERRENCE

At the end of World War II in 1945, the United States was the only country with the technology to make an atom bomb. But four years later, on August 29, 1949, Soviet physicists tested their own atom bomb.

At the time, the United States and the Soviet Union were competing against each other. They were the world's superpowers. The United States and its allies supported democracy. The Soviet Union and its allies supported **communism**.

Soviet army trucks pull nuclear missiles through Red Square in Moscow. Such parades demonstrated Russia's military strength.

This photograph shows an intercontinental ballistic missile (ICBM) in its silo in the United States.

The competition between the two sides was called the Cold War (1947–1991). The superpowers did not fight each other. However, they both funded other wars around the world. They also threatened each other.

MUTUAL DESTRUCTION

Both superpowers now had nuclear weapons. But they both hesitated to fire their weapons. They knew the other side would fire back. That would lead to the destruction of both countries. This was the basis of a theory called mutually assured destruction. The theory was sometimes known by its initials, MAD.

Missile Silos

Both American and Soviet scientists designed missile silos. These were deep underground pits that held intercontinental ballistic missiles. The missiles carried nuclear warheads. The silos were lined with hardened concrete and could withstand all but a direct hit. Even after an attack, their crews could fire back at the enemy.

Facilities such as this underground control desk would allow operators to launch missile attacks even after an attack on the United States.

NUCLEAR ARMS RACE

No defense would stop a nuclear attack, so both sides tried to prevent an attack before it took place. That meant persuading the enemy that launching an attack would lead to its own destruction. Both sides developed a range of nuclear weapons and ways to fire them. Both had nuclear weapons on long-range bombers and on ships or submarines. There were missiles in underground silos and on mobile launchers.

There was no chance of destroying all these weapons in a surprise attack. Whichever side was attacked would have nuclear weapons left to launch an attack of its own. The chance of winning a nuclear war was so small it was not worth the risk of going to war in the first place.

In the 1980s, US scientists developed the Strategic Defense Initiative. They planned to put lasers on satellites in space. The lasers would shoot down missiles fired at the United States. International treaties now ban putting weapons in space and scientists are busy planning a new generation of Earth-based weapons.

SDI planned to put lasers on satellites in orbit around Earth. The technology was never built, and some scientists believe it would not have worked.

SCIENCE FILE

Star Wars

In 1983 US President Ronald Reagan launched the Strategic Defense Initiative. It was also known as SDI or Star Wars. Planners aimed to put lasers on satellites. The lasers would shoot down Soviet missiles in the air. The SDI was never built, but it helped cause the collapse of the Soviet Union in 1990. The Soviets could not keep up with US military spending.

TIMELINE

c. 700 BCE   The crossbow is invented in China.

214 BCE   The ancient Greek scientist Archimedes develops weapons to protect the port of Syracuse from attack by Roman ships.

c. 1200   The first guns are invented in China.

c. 1200   The first longbows appear in Wales. They are longer and more powerful than ordinary bows.

c. 1400   English armies use the longbow in battles against the French.

c. 1520   The German Augustus Kotter invents rifling, grooves inside a gun barrel that cause a bullet to spin, making it fly straighter. Rifling becomes common in the 1800s.

1805   William Congreve invents the Congreve rocket, based on weapons used in India.

1861   Richard Gatling invents an early machine gun, the Gatling gun.

1866   Robert Whitehead invents a torpedo that is driven through the water by a small propeller turned by compressed air.

1879   Armor-piercing Palliser shot sinks an ironclad warship for the first time in a battle between Chile and Peru.

1883   Hiram Maxim invents the Maxim gun, which can fire up to 550 rounds per minute, and which automatically reloads as it ejects a used shell.

1916	British physicists invent the depth charge for use against German U-boats, or submarines, during World War I.
1941	Clarence Hickman invents the bazooka, a rocket launcher that can be carried and used by an individual infantry soldier.
1942	The Germans begin using the V-1 rocket in attacks on Britain, France, and Belgium.
1944	The Germans fire V-2 rockets in long-distance attacks on London.
1945	On July 16, the first atom bomb is tested in New Mexico. On August 6 a US bomber drops an atom bomb on the Japanese city of Hiroshima, starting a new age of nuclear weaponry.
1949	The Soviet Union develops an atom bomb, beginning an arms race with the United States.
1960	US engineer Theodore H. Maiman builds the first laser. Engineers use the laser to target missiles and as an alternative to radar.
1983	The United States announces the Strategic Defense Initiative, a program to put lasers on satellites in space. SDI is never built.
2008	An airborne laser weapon is fired for the first time from an aicraft in flight.

GLOSSARY

armorers: people who make weapons or armor

artillery: large guns such as cannons

ballistic missiles: missiles that travel in a high arc before falling onto their targets under gravity

cartridge: a case containing a bullet and gunpowder to make it fire

chain reaction: a chemical reaction in which each step of the process leads to further reactions

communism: a political system in which everything is owned by the state

colonial: relating to colonies, or areas a country rules in other lands

cruise missile: a low-flying missile steered by an onboard computer

detonated: caused to explode

element: a chemical substance that cannot be broken down into other substances

fortifications: walls and barriers built to defend a place from attack

fulcrum: a pivot point around which a lever turns

kinetic energy: the energy of motion

matter: all physical substances

missiles: weapons that are propelled toward a target

muskets: guns with long barrels

propeller: a device with turning blades that propels ships or aircraft

radioactive: producing a dangerous form of energy called radiation

siege: a military operation to capture a town or castle by surrounding it

Soviet: from or having to do with the Soviet Union, a nation that existed from 1922 to 1991, based in modern-day Russia

volley: a number of bullets fired at the same time

warheads: the explosive heads of missiles

waterline: the level reached by water on the side of a ship

FURTHER RESOURCES

Books

Roesler, Jill. *Eyewitness to the Dropping of the Atomic Bombs*. Mankato, MN: Child's World, 2016.

Samuels, Charlie. *Machines and Weaponry of World War I*. New York: Gareth Stevens, 2013.

Rooney, Ann. *The History of Physics*. New York: Rosen, 2013.

Wyckoff, Edwin Brit. *The Man Who Invented the Laser: The Genius of Theodore H. Maiman*. Berkeley Heights, NJ: Enslow Elementary, 2014.

Websites

Archery Facts
http://www.softschools.com /facts/sports/archery_facts /787/

Archimedes and his Discoveries
http://easyscienceforkids.com /all-about-archimedes/

The Machine Gun
http://spartacus-educational .com/FWWmachinegun.htm

SDI (Star Wars)
http://www.american-historama .org/1945-1989-cold-war-era /strategic-defense-initiative.htm

What Is a Rocket?
https://www.nasa.gov/audience /forstudents/k-4/stories/nasa -knows/what-is-a-rocket-k4 .html

World War II: The Atomic Bomb
http://www.ducksters.com /history/world_war_ii/ww2 _atomic_bomb.php

INDEX